SHAPED BY SCRIPTURE

I Lift My Eyes to the Hills

PSALMS

ALEX VARUGHESE

Cover and Interior Design: J. R. Caines
Layout: Jeff Gifford

All Scripture quotations, unless indicated, are taken from THE HOLY BIBLE, NEW INTERNATIONAL VERSION®, NIV® Copyright © 1973, 1978, 1984, 2011 by Biblica, Inc.® Used by permission. All rights reserved worldwide.

Scriptures marked (ESV) are taken from The Holy Bible, English Standard Version (esv), copyright © 2001 by Crossway Bibles, a division of Good News Publishers. Used by permission. All rights reserved.

The internet addresses, email addresses, and phone numbers in this book are accurate at the time of publication. They are provided as a resource. The Foundry Publishing does not endorse them or vouch for their content or permanence.

Contents

THE *SHAPED BY SCRIPTURE* SERIES

The first step of an organized study of the Bible is the selection of a biblical book that a reader plans to study. Often people pick a book they are most familiar with, or books they consider as easy to understand, or books that, according to popular opinion, have more relevance to Christians today than other books of the Bible. However, it is important to recognize the truth that God's Word is not limited to a few books. All the biblical books, both individually and collectively, communicate God's Word to us. As Paul affirms in 2 Timothy 3:16, "All Scripture is God-breathed and is useful for teaching, rebuking, correcting and training in righteousness." We interpret the term "God-breathed" to mean inspired by God. If Christians are going to take 2 Timothy 3:16 seriously, then we should all set the goal of encountering God's Word as communicated through all sixty-six books of the Bible. New Christians or those with little to no prior knowledge of the Bible might find it best to start with a New Testament book like 1 John, James, or the Gospel of John.

By purchasing this volume, you have chosen to study the book of Psalms. You've made a great choice because this book of poetry and songs has been a favorite of Christians throughout history. Psalms offers words of comfort, assurance, and hope, as well as instructions and admonitions that are fitting for all of life's circumstances. Moreover, this book offers the people of God eloquent examples of prayers for all occasions. Because the goal of this series is to illustrate a holistic method of studying the Bible rather than a comprehensive study of an entire book, our study will be limited to seven psalms that represent the different types of psalms found in the Bible.

How This Study Works

This Bible study is intended for a period of seven weeks. We have chosen a specific passage for each week's study. This study can be done individually or with a small group.

For individual study, we recommend a five-day study each week, following the guidelines given below:

1	On the first day of the study, read the relevant passage several times until you become fully familiar with the verses, words, and phrases.
2	On the second day, we will review the setting and organization of the passage.
3	On the third day, we will observe some of the realities portrayed in the passage.
4	On the fourth day, we will investigate the relationship of the individual passage to the larger story of God in the Bible.
5	On the fifth day, we will reflect on the function of the story as we hear it today, the invitation it extends to us, and our response to God, who speaks through God's Word.

If this Bible study is done as a group activity, we recommend that members of the group meet together on the sixth day to share and discuss what they have learned from God's Word and how it has transformed their lives.

You may want to have a study Bible to give you additional insights as we work through the book of Psalms. Other helpful resources are *Discovering the Old Testament* and the *New Beacon Bible Commentary* volumes on Psalms: *Psalms 1—72* and *Psalms 73—150*.

Literary Forms in the Bible

There are several literary forms represented throughout the Bible. The divinely inspired writers used various techniques to communicate God's Word to their ancient audiences. The major literary forms (also known as genres) of the Bible are:

- narratives

- laws

- history

- Wisdom literature (in the form of dialogues and proverbial statements)

- poetry (consisting of poems of praise, lament, trust in God, and more)

- prophecy

- discourses

- parables

- miracle stories

- letters (also known as epistles)

- exhortations

- apocalyptic writings

Within each of these forms, one may find subgenres. Each volume in the *Shaped by Scripture* series will briefly overview the genres found in the book of the Bible that is the subject of that study.

When biblical writers utilized a particular literary form, they intended for it to have a specific effect on their audience. This concept can be understood by examining genres that are familiar to us in our contemporary setting. For example, novels that are comedies inspire good and happy feelings in their readers; tragedies, on the other hand, are meant to induce sorrow. What is true of the intended effect of literary forms in contemporary literature is also true of literary forms found in the Bible.

THE BOOK OF PSALMS

The book of Psalms (sometimes also called the Psalter), is a collection of sacred hymns that were used by the ancient Israelites in their temple worship. Its Hebrew title is *Tehillim*, which means "praises." This describes much of the book's content. The Greek title is *Psalmoi*, which means "songs that are sung to the accompaniment of musical instruments."

The headings of a number of psalms contain references to their use on special days or occasions (see 30, 38, 70, 92, 100). The book of Psalms is one of the most quoted Old Testament books in the New Testament (the New Testament includes fifty-five quotations from thirty-five different psalms). Various New Testament books record Jesus citing psalms (Matthew 5:5, 34–35; 6:26; 7:23; 27:46), and New Testament writers apply quotations of the psalms to Jesus's life and ministry (see, for example, Acts 2:25–28; 13:33; Hebrews 2:6–8). The singing of psalms has been a regular part of worship in the Christian church throughout the centuries, and continues to be so in churches that follow a formal liturgy. In non-liturgical churches that follow the lectionary reading program, the psalms are also a regular part of scripture reading. The book remains an important source for teaching and preaching, Bible study, and the nurturing of spiritual life in the church.

Who Wrote Psalms?

The fact that there are 150 psalms in the book shows that psalm-writing was a common practice in Israel; however, we do not know when this practice began, who collected the psalms, or how they became a part of the book we see in our Bible today. The authorship of many of the psalms is also uncertain. The headings that precede most of the psalms (all but thirty-four of them) contain different notations, including the names of people who may have composed them. The most common names are David (74 psalms), Asaph (12 psalms) and the sons of Korah (11 psalms). Other names include Heman, Ethan, Jeduthun, Solomon, and Moses.

Scholars think that originally the psalms were part of five smaller books (chapters 1–41, 42–72, 73–89, 90–106, 107–150) which were later merged into one book. They cite as evidence the ending of each book with a shorter or longer version of a praise statement (see 41:13; 72:19–20; 89:52; 106:48; 150:6).

Though psalms were composed by various individuals for use in the temple worship, some psalms were intended to be used by individual worshipers and others by the worshiping community as a whole. This is evident in the use of both first-person singular ("I") and first-person plural pronouns ("we," "us") in the psalms. Worship in Israel was primarily an individual act; the community gathered together for worship only on specially designated festival and celebration times and in times of national calamities such as defeat in war, natural disasters, etc.

Genres

The headings found in most of the psalms include terms that indicate their literary genre. Song (sir or *mizmor*) is the most common designation (87 psalms). Thirteen psalms are called didactic songs (*maskil*). Other labels include golden poem (*miktam*; 6 psalms), prayer (*tephilla*; 5 psalms), penitential song (*shiggayon*; 1 psalm), and praise (*tehilla*; 1 psalm). The term "a song of ascents" is found in the headings of Psalms 120–134. Psalms 111–118 and 146–150 are traditionally called Hallel psalms because they all (except 114 and 118) begin and/or end with the phrase "hallelujah" ("Praise the Lord"). Some modern commentators classify the psalms under two categories: praise hymns and laments. Others expand the praise hymns to include hymns proper, thanksgiving psalms, psalms of trust and confidence, royal psalms, wisdom psalms, liturgical psalms, and historical psalms. The following is a brief explanation of the characteristics of the sub-genres this study will cover, as well as the songs of ascent.

Hymns

These psalms make up about one-fifth of the book, and their primary objective is to praise God. Some praise him for his kingship (for example, Psalms 93 and 96), or for choosing Zion/Jerusalem as his earthly dwelling place (for example, Psalms 46 and 48). Others give no specific reason for the praise (for example, Psalms 8, 29, 33).

Psalms of Thanksgiving

These psalms often begin with the call to give thanks (Psalms 105–107). Psalms which may not begin with this call, but focus on thanksgiving, also belong to this sub-genre (see Psalms 9, 30, 66, 92, 116, 118, 138). The inspiration behind these psalms may have been an answer to prayer or God's deliverance of an individual or the worshiping community. These psalms usually contain some reference to the crisis that prompted the prayer for deliverance.

Psalms of Trust and Confidence

These psalms convey an individual's or the worshiping community's confidence that God is their deliverer, provider, and the source of their hope and strength. Psalm 23 is an excellent example of these psalms, which are characterized by language of trust and confidence (see Psalms 3, 4, 11, 16, 115, 125). Such expressions in the setting of public worship were perhaps meant to be a testimony and an encouragement to others to put their trust in God.

Royal Psalms

Psalms that focus on God's rule over Israel through Davidic kings are known as royal psalms (see Psalms 2, 18, 20, 21, 45, 72, 101, 110, 144). These psalms recall and reflect on God's covenant promises to David (see 2 Samuel 7:12–16). An important characteristic of these psalms is the reference to the Davidic king as "the anointed one" (Hebrew *mashiach*; see 2:2). Some of these psalms may have been used during coronation rituals (see Psalms 2, 21, 72, 101, and 110). Psalm 18 is a prayer by the king; psalm 20 is a prayer for the king. Psalm 45 was perhaps composed for use in a royal wedding ceremony. The early Christian church interpreted the royal psalms in light of the ministry, suffering, death, and resurrection of Jesus (see Matthew 22:44; Acts 2:34; 1 Corinthians 15:25; Ephesians 1:20; Hebrews 1:13). For this reason, these psalms have become known as the "messianic psalms" in the church.

Wisdom Psalms

A number of psalms focus on the distinction between the righteous and the wicked and the importance of maintaining a proper relationship with God by following the path of righteousness. This is an emphasis found in the wisdom books in the Old Testament (Proverbs, Ecclesiastes, and Job). These psalms may also be called instruction psalms because of their emphasis that the law (*torah*) is the guide to the path of righteousness. Psalms 1, 19, 37, 49, 73, 112, 119, 127, 128, and 133 are examples of this type of psalm. A number of these psalms are structured as beatitudes—blessings or happiness pronounced upon those who live a Torah-centered life (1, 112, 119, 128). Some of these psalms contain exhortations, warnings, and assertions which teach about the destinies of the wicked and the good.

Psalms of Lament

More than 50 psalms belong to a category referred to as "laments" or "prayers for help." These psalms express the anguish, bitterness, disappointment, and frustration of the Israelite worshiping community. Some of these are an individual's laments (indicated by the first person singular "I"), and others are laments of the worshiping community ("we," "us").

Psalms of Ascent

Psalms or songs of ascent, also called pilgrim psalms (Psalms 120–134), were most likely sung by Israelite pilgrims as they climbed the steps of the temple or journeyed to Jerusalem to participate in the annual festivals. The word "ascents" comes from a verb that means "to go up," and suggests the going up to the temple at Mount Zion/Jerusalem to worship God.

Study and Interpretation

The interpretation of a psalm requires us to know its literary characteristics and particular emphases. Before we proceed, let us look at some features that are shared by all the psalms.

Psalms are poetry, and the book of Psalms is the best example of Hebrew poetry in the Bible. The heading of a psalm usually indicates one or more of the following details: authorship, genre, historical context, instruction to the musicians, or instructions for use on special occasions (see the heading of Psalm 54, which includes all of these details except instructions for its use). In Hebrew, the poetic lines of psalms have a rhythmic quality and are meant to be sung or chanted. Most of the psalms' poetic features are not evident in English translations. However, an important literary feature that is recognizable in English is parallelism—a linguistic structure in which words, phrases, and thoughts expressed in the first line of a verse correspond in some way to the second line. Often, the second line may repeat the idea of the first line, or expand it, or introduce a contrasting idea. Recognizing instances of parallelism is important for understanding a psalm's meaning. Symbolic language, alliteration, and acrostics (in which each new verse begins with a letter of the Hebrew alphabet in descending order) are some other poetic techniques we see in the Hebrew text.

Now, let us look at some specific guidelines to keep in mind when we engage in the study of a psalm:

1. The book of Psalms is composed of individual psalms; thus, we should refrain from thinking of them as chapters in the book.

2. Each psalm is intended to be heard, sung, or studied in its entirety. As you absorb the words of the psalm, trace its structure and development: How does it begin? How does it end? What is its main focus?

3. Each psalm is composed of human words addressed to God, and as such, may be a praise, a thanksgiving, an expression of trust in God, an instruction, a prayer for help, an entrance hymn, or a proclamation of God's kingship and rule over the world through the Davidic king.

4. Psalms are also God's word to us: words of comfort, assurance, hope, instruction, warning, and more.

5. Carefully observe how the psalmists portray God: he is often described as the defender, deliverer, comforter, provider, sustainer, and the source of strength and hope for all who trust in him.

6. Some psalms contain words of hatred, curse the psalmist's enemies, and appeal to God for judgment. This reflects the Israelites' belief in God's righteous judgment on his people's enemies. The New Testament's command to love our enemies should guide our interpretation of these prayers for God's judgment.

7. It is important to understand the historical context and purpose of psalms that refer to the Messiah (a term that means "the anointed one") before we relate them to the life and works of Jesus the Messiah.

8. The New Testament writers' allusions to psalms do not indicate that they understood the psalms as prophecies; rather, they were relating the psalmists' words to some aspect of Jesus's earthly life and works.

9. When properly understood, psalms can become lenses through which we see our world today. They reveal that our world, like the psalmists', is filled with a strange mixture of joy and sorrow, praise and complaint, fear and hope, doubt and trust.

Major Theological Themes

Martin Luther called the book of Psalms "a little Bible" because it encapsulates all the Bible's themes, including creation, sin, judgment, and salvation. There are a few key theological themes that are especially emphasized in the Psalms:

God is the sovereign Creator. Belief in God as the sovereign Creator is fundamental to the psalmists' understanding of God (see Psalms 93 and 104).

God is King, and his rule is sovereign. God is not only creator, but also sovereign ruler over all creation. God's kingship is a primary theme in a number of psalms (Psalms 47, 93, 95-99).

God has characteristics we can know and trust. The psalmists frequently describe the essential characteristics of God the creator. Chief among them are his greatness (Psalm 145), majesty (Psalm 97), power (Psalm 76), holiness (Psalm 99), righteousness and justice (Psalm 71), faithfulness (Psalm 8), covenant loyalty/ steadfast love (Psalm 136), and mercy (Psalm 103).

God is our Savior. God the creator also saves his people from their enemies and nations that threaten them. His power to save is an emphasis in Psalms 3, 47, 68, and 98.

God is the sovereign Judge. God's kingship is the basis for the psalmists' conviction that he judges individuals, nations, other gods, and even his own people, making things right throughout the earth (see Psalms 9, 10, 50, 94, 96).

God is the provider and sustainer of all creation. Psalm 104 is a praise of the God who not only created the heavens and the earth, but also sustains all creation with his provision.

Humanity is subject to God. Humanity's dignity as creatures made in God's image, their fragility and sinfulness, and their destiny are themes found in Psalms 8, 90, and 103.

Israel is God's covenant people. A number of psalms focus on God's deliverance of Israel, his choice to make them his people, and his continued care for them, even in the midst of their rebellion and sin against him. Psalmists often use shepherd-sheep imagery to describe God-Israel relationship (Psalms 44, 74, 77, 78, 80, 105, 106).

The Davidic Messiah is coming. Some psalms describe God's rule over the nations and his people through his "anointed one" (*messiah*), the king who sits on the throne of David. God's covenant with David (2 Samuel 7:11-16; see Psalms 89, 132) is the basis for this belief (Psalms 2, 18, 20, 21, 22, 45, 72, 110).

Zion is the city of God. God's earthly dwelling place, the temple located in Zion, is significant in a number of psalms. This is the city from where God rules the world (Psalms 46, 48, 84, 87) and to which God's faithful people go to worship him (Psalms 43:3-4; 122).

God's instructions are law. Emphasis on God's law (*torah*), his instructions for Israel's salvation and blessedness, and Israel's faithful relationship with God is found in a number of psalms, most importantly in Psalms 1, 19, and 119.

God will judge the righteous and the wicked. The psalms make a clear distinction between the righteous (those who live on God's terms) and the wicked (those who live by self-rule, apart from God). The psalmists grappled with the prosperity of the wicked, but also saw this success as temporary. They believed in God's care and protection for the righteous and the eventual destruction of the wicked (for example, see Psalms 1, 5, 7, 10, 17).

PSALM 8

This is the first hymn of praise in Psalms. There is no call to worship such as, "Sing to the LORD," or "Praise the LORD," as we see in a number of other praise psalms. Instead, this psalm begins with a proclamation of God's majesty. The language throughout the psalm draws heavily on the creation story in Genesis 1.

The psalm begins with a heading which contains a brief note to the director of music, or choirmaster. The phrase "According to gittith" is most likely a musical term. Some commentators think the word gittith comes from *gat*, which means "wine press." They suggest that this term instructs the choirmaster to direct the singing of this psalm to the tune of "a song of the wine press." Still, this term's exact meaning remains unclear to us.

The other part of the heading, the phrase "A psalm of David," indicates its authorship. "Of David" in Hebrew is *ledavid*, which literally means "to/for David." Most commentators think psalms that contain "of David" in their headings were dedicated to David, attributed to David, or written for him by a psalm writer. Thus, we are not sure whether David himself wrote this psalm.

Since the authorship of psalms is an unresolvable question, most commentators use the term "the psalmist" rather than "David" or another name that might be found in the headings of psalms. We will follow that practice throughout this study.

WEEK 1, DAY 1

Absorb the passage in Psalm 8 by reading it aloud several times until you become familiar with its verses, words, and phrases. Imagine you are worshiping in the ancient Jerusalem temple as you listen to this song of praise.

WEEK 1, DAY 2
PSALM 8

The Setting

It is possible that this psalm was sung by the worshiping community in ancient Israel (see "our LORD" in verse 1), though it may have been originally composed by the psalmist as his own praise of God (see the first-person singular "I" in verse 3). We cannot ascertain the specific occasion of its use in the temple worship. However, its literary context reveals the important role it plays in the book. This psalm follows three lament psalms that contain prayers for God's salvation (Psalms 5, 6, 7). The description of humans' royal status preceded by a prayer for God's help demonstrates that though humans are rulers appointed by God, they have no power to save themselves from their troubles. The psalmist acknowledges that humans are still creatures, and as such, they need God's salvation.

When we place this psalm in its ancient cultural context, we find a sharp contrast between the Israelites' view of humans and the ancient Mesopotamians' view. Creation accounts from ancient Mesopotamian cultures portray humans as being created to do menial tasks for the gods and live a life of suffering. These cultures did not affirm the dignity or worth of humans that this psalm celebrates.

The Organization

Psalm 8 begins and ends with the same enthusiastic proclamation of praise. These praise statements bookend the psalmist's reflections about God the creator and humans, his appointed stewards of the earth.

To discover the message of Psalm 8, let's divide it into five sections. **Below, summarize or paraphrase the general message or theme of each grouping of verses (following the pattern provided for 8:1a and 8:1b–2).**

1. Psalm 8:1a

An exuberant shout of praise celebrates the majesty of God's name that is seen all over

the earth.

2. Psalm 8:1b–2

God silences his enemies through the praises of the weak and powerless.

3. Psalm 8:3–4

4. Psalm 8:5–8

5. Psalm 8:9

WEEK 1, DAY 3

What's Happening in the Passage?

As we read through these passages, there are certain ideas and words that were familiar to the original readers, but are not as familiar to us. Two thousand years and a vastly different culture obscure some of these ideas from us today. You may encounter some of these words and ideas in your study today. Some of them have been explained in more detail in the **Word Study Notes**. If you want even more detail, you can supplement this study with a Bible dictionary or commentary.

1. Psalm 8:1a

The psalmist addresses God as the LORD our Lord[1] and praises the majesty[2] of God's name[3] which is seen throughout the earth.

2. Psalm 8:1b–2

The psalmist acknowledges that God's glory extends above the heavens.[1] He describes the praises of the weak and vulnerable[2] as a powerful weapon with which God defends his glory and silences his enemies.[3]

WORD STUDY NOTES #1

[1] LORD (*Yahweh*) is the personal name of Israel's God. Their use of this name indicates their belief in his power as the Creator of the heavens and the earth. He revealed himself to Israel as their redeemer and covenant maker. Lord (*Adonai*) is a royal title—an address to a king or a master. English translations of Scripture have varied the capitalization style of the word "Lord" to give us hints about when the Hebrew was using *Yahweh* (LORD) and when *Adonai* (Lord).

[2] "Majestic" is a term used to address a king and implies the ruler's strength, power, and fame.

[3] References to "God's name" are used to encompass the essence of who God is—his character, power, strength, and other attributes.

WORD STUDY NOTES #2

[1] In the Hebrew text, what has been translated into English as "in the heavens" is literally "above the heavens."

[2] Children and infants represent the weak, the vulnerable, and the powerless in the world. Here, they are the ones who worship God in a world that is hostile to God.

[3] God's enemies are the forces that are hostile to God's sovereign and good purpose for his creation. The Old Testament depicts God's enemies in figurative or mythical terms such as the sea (Psalm 74:13), a sea monster (Psalm 74:13), Leviathan the gliding serpent (Isaiah 27:1), the waters (Psalm 104:6), and more. Psalmists also describe the enemies of God's people as the enemies of God himself (Psalm 92:9).

WORD STUDY NOTES #3

[1]"What is mankind" is not a question about the hopeless condition of humans, but a reflective question about humanity's true identity.

[2]In the Hebrew text, "human beings" is literally "son of man," meaning a mortal, transient, weak, earthly creature.

[3]The terms "mindful" and "care for" indicate God's awareness of and attentiveness to the needs of humans, who are mortal by nature.

WORD STUDY NOTES #4

[1]In the Hebrew text, "a little lower than the angels" is literally "a little lower than God." The Hebrew noun *'elohim*, a common name for God in the Old Testament, means "heavenly beings," which is implied by the word "angels" in the NIV translation.

[2]"Put everything under their feet" is an expression of royal authority, not of subjugation.

WORD STUDY NOTES #5

[1]The conclusion of the psalm with a repetition of the opening shout of praise indicates that the psalmist's objective was not to glorify humans, but to praise the God who appointed them as rulers over all creation.

Create your own brief summary or description of the realities portrayed in verses 3–4, 5–8, and 9.

3. Psalm 8:3–4[1, 2, 3]

_____

_____

_____

_____

_____

_____

4. Psalm 8:5–8[1, 2]

_____

_____

_____

_____

_____

_____

_____

5. Psalm 8:9[1]

_____

_____

_____

_____

_____

_____

_____

Discoveries

Let's summarize our discoveries from Psalm 8.

1. The psalmist enthusiastically proclaims the majesty of God's name — his strength, power, character, and attributes — as seen throughout creation.

2. God, the majestic Creator, remembers humans' weak and transient condition and uses their praises as a powerful defense against his enemies.

3. God bestowed royal status upon humans by appointing them as rulers over all creation.

4. Though God granted humans royal status, the psalmist does not praise them; instead, he implies that humans should praise God through the faithful fulfillment of their God-given vocations.

If you have a study Bible, it may have references in a margin, a middle column, or footnotes that point to other biblical texts. You may find it helpful in understanding how the whole story of God ties together to look up some of those other scriptures from time to time.

Hymnic Psalms and the Story of God

Whenever we read a biblical text, it is important to ask how it relates to the rest of the Bible. Praise of God, which is the primary focus of this psalm, is an emphasis in a number of other psalms, as well as in biblical passages about worship. Creation, the human condition, and humanity's exalted place in God's creation are also the focus of a number of biblical passages. **In the space provided, write a short summary of how the themes of praising God and humanity's role on earth are reflected in each passage.**

1. Genesis 1:26–28

_____

_____

_____

_____

_____

_____

_____

2. Job 7:17–18

_____

_____

_____

_____

_____

_____

_____

_____

_____

3. Psalm 89:5–18

4. Psalm 103

5. Psalm 135

6. Psalm 146

_____

7. Matthew 21:15–16

_____

8. 1 Corinthians 1:26–31

_____

9. Hebrews 2:6–9

_____

WEEK 1, DAY 5

Psalms and Our World Today

When we look at the theme of praise in Psalm 8, it can become the lens through which we see ourselves, our world, and God's action in our world today. As a praise psalm, it exposes to us the missing elements in our praise of God. It also reveals to us our true identity, though we often attempt to define it based on our professions and accomplishments. The psalmist's question of who deserves our praise is a critical challenge to the readers of this psalm who live in a world of prideful and idolatrous worship of the self and others. Let us take a closer look at our world, ourselves, our worship, and God through the lens of this psalm.

1. What does Psalm 8 reveal to us about the nature of our worship of God today?

Our praise of God is often focused on what God does for us; we seldom think of the wonder of creation as a reason for our regular worship of God.

Following the above example, answer these questions about how we can understand our world, God's action, and ourselves.

2. How would most people answer the question, "What is humanity?"

3. How would most people respond to the idea that God remembers them and knows their needs?

4. How would most people in our world define their identity?

_____

_____

_____

_____

_____

_____

_____

5. How would our world respond to the psalmist's view of humans as divinely appointed shepherd-stewards of creation?

_____

_____

_____

_____

_____

_____

_____

_____

_____

6. What does this psalm say to a world that often engages in self-praise and praise of
other people?

_____

_____

_____

_____

_____

_____

_____

_____

_____

Invitation and Response

God's Word always invites a response. Think about the way the themes of worship, creation, praise of God, and the role of humanity speak to us today. How does Psalm 8 invite us to respond?

_____

_____

_____

_____

_____

_____

_____

_____

_____

_____

_____

Praying the psalms is an important and meaningful spiritual discipline. Write your own prayer of praise using ideas and words found in Psalm 8.

_____

_____

_____

_____

_____

_____

_____

_____

_____

_____

_____

The majesty of
God's name is seen
throughout creation.

PSALM 116

Psalm 116 is a song of thanksgiving. It lacks a heading; it also lacks the call to "give thanks" that appears in a number of other thanksgiving psalms (see 105, 106, 107, 118). Though the Hebrew Bible preserves this as a single psalm, it may have previously existed as two psalms; in the Greek and Latin Bibles, 116:1–9 appears as Psalm 114, and 116:10–19 as Psalm 115. The psalm's unity is evident in the recurring themes of calling on the name of the LORD (vv. 2, 4, 13, 17) and of God delivering the psalmist from death (vv. 3, 8, 15).

In later Jewish tradition, this psalm became a part of "the Egyptian Hallel" (Psalms 113–118), which was sung during the Passover meal in remembrance of God's deliverance of Israel from Egypt. In Christian tradition, this psalm has long been part of the Scripture reading during the celebration of the LORD's Supper on Maundy Thursday. This tradition may originate in Jesus taking the cup and giving thanks before he offered it to his disciples during his last Passover meal with them (Mark 14:23–25).

WEEK 2, DAY 1

Absorb the passage in Psalm 116 by reading it aloud several times until you become familiar with its verses, words, and phrases.

WEEK 2, DAY 2

PSALM 116

The Setting

Originally, this song of thanksgiving was sung by an individual worshiper who prayed for God's help and salvation during a life-threatening situation (vv. 3–4). We read that God heard his prayer and saved him from death (vv. 1, 6, 8, 16). The psalm indicates that the worshiper vowed to offer a thank offering to God (vv. 13–14, 17–19), and the fulfillment of this vow in the temple was the occasion for this song. As he came to the temple with his offering and song, he testified to the worshiping community about the graciousness of God (v. 5). It is possible that this psalm became a song of thanksgiving for all faithful people in Israel who had experienced God's deliverance.

The Organization

The structure of Psalm 116 is straightforward: the psalmist begins with an expression of devotion to the God who heard his cry for help, and ends with his commitment to show his gratitude in the setting of public worship. Other themes include the threat of death and the psalmist's promise to serve God and proclaim his salvation.

To discover the message of Psalm 116, let's divide it into eight sections. **Below, summarize or paraphrase the general message or theme of each grouping of verses (following the pattern provided for 116:1–2, 3–4, 5–7, and 15-16).**

1. Psalm 116:1–2

The psalmist proclaims his devotion to the God who heard his cry for mercy.

2. Psalm 116:3–4

The psalmist prays for God to rescue him from the threat of death.

3. Psalm 116:5–7

The psalmist celebrates God's goodness.

4. Psalm 116:8–9

5. Psalm 116:10–11

6. Psalm 116:12–14

_____
_____
_____
_____
_____
_____
_____
_____
_____
_____
_____

7. Psalm 116:15–16

The psalmist commits to serve the God who rescued him from death.

8. Psalm 116:17–19

_____
_____
_____
_____
_____
_____
_____
_____
_____
_____
_____
_____
_____
_____

WEEK 2, DAY 3

What's Happening in the Passage?

As we read through these passages, there are certain ideas and words that were familiar to the original readers, but are not as familiar to us. Two thousand years and a vastly different culture obscure some of these ideas from us today. You may encounter some of these words and ideas in your study today. Some of them have been explained in more detail in the **Word Study Notes**. If you want even more detail, you can supplement this study with a Bible dictionary or commentary.

1. Psalm 116:1–2

The psalmist proclaims his love[1] for the LORD, who answered his cry for mercy—he has experienced God's love in action. God demonstrated his attentiveness to the psalmist; in response, the psalmist makes a lifelong commitment to worship God.

_____

_____

_____

_____

_____

2. Psalm 116:3–4

The psalmist is at the point of death and anxious about the grave that awaits him. His impending death fills him with sorrow,[1] and he prays to God seeking deliverance.[2]

_____

_____

_____

_____

_____

WORD STUDY NOTES #1

[1] The word for "love" in Hebrew ('ahab) expresses the idea of the devotion, commitment, and support found in a family relationship. This is also the word that is used to describe God's love for his people. Love for God is expressed only rarely in the psalms (see 5:11; 31:23), and Psalm 18 is the only other psalm that begins with such an expression of love (though a different Hebrew is used). Elsewhere, the psalmist speaks of his love for God's law/instruction (119:97).

WORD STUDY NOTES #2

[1] More so than death itself, the psalmist may fear being cast out of God's presence forever.

[2] In the Old Testament, "calling on the name of God" indicates the act of worship. Here, it means praying to God with a specific appeal in the context of worship. God's name reflects his power, his will to save, and his compassion and mercy.

WORD STUDY NOTES #3

[1] Here, "the unwary" means the powerless.

[2] In Israel's thinking, the "soul" (Hebrew *nephesh*) is not something a human has or a component of an individual, but who she or he is—the whole person, or the totality of their existence.

[3] "Return to your rest" most likely means to return to a resting place where relief and security can be found—that is, God's presence in the temple.

WORD STUDY NOTES #4

[1] "Walk before the LORD" conveys a faithful relationship with God characterized by humility, praise, integrity in one's words and actions, and upright conduct.

[2] "The land of the living" is the opposite of *Sheol*, the land of the dead. It is where God's faithful people witness and experience God's saving actions.

WORD STUDY NOTES #5

[1] "In my alarm I said, 'Everyone is a liar'" is difficult to understand. It may mean that even in his frightened state, the psalmist did not seek human help because he believed that human beings cannot fulfill their promises.

3. Psalm 116:5-7

God answered the psalmist's prayer for help and saved him from death. The psalmist testifies to God's graciousness, righteousness, compassion, and protection of the powerless.[1] He also views his salvation as evidence of God's power to save those who are brought low by difficult circumstances. The psalmist's experience of God's goodness prompts him[2] to go to the temple, where he can enjoy rest[3] and freedom from his fear of death.

Create your own brief summary or description of the realities portrayed in verses 8–9, 10–11, 12–14, 15–16, and 17–19.

4. Psalm 116:8–9[1, 2]

_____

_____

_____

_____

_____

_____

5. Psalm 116:10–11[1]

_____

_____

_____

_____

_____

_____

_____

_____

6. Psalm 116:12–14[1, 2]

_____

_____

_____

_____

_____

_____

_____

7. Psalm 116:15–16[1, 2]

_____

_____

_____

_____

_____

_____

_____

8. Psalm 116:17–19[1, 2, 3]

_____

_____

_____

_____

_____

_____

_____

WORD STUDY NOTES #6

[1] "The cup of salvation" probably refers to pouring a drink offering during a thanksgiving ritual to celebrate God's saving action (see Exodus 25:29; 29:40; Numbers 28:7).

[2] In the Old Testament, when people prayed for God's help in times of crisis, they often made pledges that they would fulfill upon God's answer to their prayers (see Genesis 28:20-22; 1 Samuel 1:11). We do not know the specific vows the psalmist made when he prayed for God's help.

WORD STUDY NOTES #7

[1] "Precious" here means "costly" or "grievous," which conveys a sense of a great loss. Death silences the praise of the believer and their witness to God's faithfulness. According to Psalm 6:5, there is no praise of God from the grave.

[2] Some commentators think the phrase "the son of your maidservant"(ESV) conveys the idea of a bondservant or household slave.

WORD STUDY NOTES #8

[1] See Leviticus 7:12 and 22:29 for instructions for thank offerings.

[2] "The courts of the house of the LORD" refers to the outer court of the temple where worshipers gathered to offer their sacrifices to God.

[3] "Praise the LORD" (_hallelujah_) is the response of the faithful people who witness the psalmist's testimony and the fulfillment of his vows in the temple.

Discoveries

Let's summarize our discoveries from Psalm 116.

1. The psalmist proclaims his love for God and makes a lifelong commitment to worship the God who delivered him from the threat of death.

2. The psalmist testifies about God's grace, righteousness, compassion, and protection of the helpless.

3. God's salvation prompted the psalmist to make a commitment to return to the temple, where God's presence and freedom from all anxieties can be found.

4. The psalmist believes that God delivered him from death so that he may live as a faithful witness of God's salvation in the world.

5. The psalmist affirms his commitment to offer a sacrifice, fulfill his vows, and faithfully serve the God who delivered him from death.

WEEK 2, DAY 4

Psalms of Thanksgiving and the Story of God

Whenever we read a biblical text, it is important to ask how it relates to the rest of the Bible. Thanksgiving to God, which is the primary focus of this psalm, is an emphasis in a number of other psalms and in biblical passages that deal with worship. Often expressions of thanksgiving found in the psalms also reveal serious afflictions and life-threatening situations endured by the psalmists and the people of God. The psalmist's emphasis on love for God, God's attentiveness and deliverance of those who cry out for help, God's graciousness, righteousness, compassion, and protection of the helpless, and worship and servitude to God are themes found in several biblical texts. The psalmist's experience also resonates with the Gospel accounts of Jesus's suffering, death, and deliverance from death in the resurrection. **In the space provided, write a short summary of how the themes of thanksgiving and God's love for creation are reflected in each passage.**

1. Genesis 28:20–22

_____

_____

_____

_____

_____

2. Deuteronomy 6:4–5

_____

_____

_____

_____

_____

_____

If you have a study Bible, it may have references in a margin, a middle column, or footnotes that point to other biblical texts. You may find it helpful in understanding how the whole story of God ties together to look up some of those other scriptures from time to time.

35

3. Psalm 72:12–14

4. Psalm 88:3–5, 10–11

5. Isaiah 38:11

6. Matthew 26:36–39

_____
_____
_____
_____
_____
_____
_____
_____
_____

7. Acts 2:22–28

_____
_____
_____
_____
_____
_____
_____
_____
_____

8. 1 Corinthians 11:23–26

_____
_____
_____
_____
_____
_____
_____
_____
_____

WEEK 2, DAY 5

Psalms and Our World Today

When we look at the theme of thanksgiving in Psalm 116, it can become the lens through which we see ourselves, our world, and God's action in our world today.

1. What can we learn about ourselves from Psalm 116?

Like the psalmist, we too are helpless to save ourselves from troubles and trials.

_____

_____

Following the above example, answer these questions about how we can understand our world, God's action, and ourselves.

2. How do we show our dependence on God in times of crisis?

_____

_____

_____

_____

_____

_____

_____

3. What is our perspective of our place of worship compared to the psalmist's view of the temple, which he calls his resting place (v. 7)?

_____

_____

_____

_____

_____

_____

_____

_____

38

4. How do we respond to God's goodness to us, our families, our churches, and the world around us?

_____

_____

_____

_____

_____

_____

_____

_____

_____

_____

_____

5. What are some tangible ways that we can express our gratitude to God?

_____

_____

_____

_____

_____

_____

_____

_____

_____

_____

_____

_____

Invitation and Response

God's Word always invites a response. Think about the way the themes of despair, salvation, and rescue speak to us today. How does Psalm 116 invite us to respond?

_____

_____

_____

_____

_____

_____

_____

_____

_____

_____

Praying the psalms is an important and meaningful spiritual discipline. Write your own prayer of thanksgiving using ideas and words found in Psalm 116.

_____

_____

_____

_____

_____

_____

_____

_____

_____

_____

_____

_____

The psalmist's
question of who
deserves our praise
is a critical challenge
to those who live in a
world of prideful and
idolatrous worship
of self and others.

PSALM 27

Psalm 27 is a psalm of trust and confidence in God. The heading includes the attribution "of David" (literally, "to/for David"; see the introduction to this study for further explanation of this heading). Some commentators think that this psalm was originally written as two psalms: one of trust and confidence (vv. 1–6), and one of lament (vv. 7–14). There is an appeal for help in verses 7–12, and the psalm ends with a strong affirmation of the psalmist's trust in God (vv. 13–14). Recurring words and phrases provide unity to the psalm (for example, see God as "salvation/savior" in vv. 1, 9; "enemies/foes" in vv. 2, 12; "heart" in vv. 3, 8, 14; "seek" in vv. 4, 8; and "life" in vv. 4, 13). The psalmist expresses trust in God in the midst of enemy attacks and opposition. While he is confident of God's presence and protection, the psalmist also knows that hostile people mean him harm, and that he needs God's help and protection. His trust in God is the only thing that enables him to face opposition and enemies, to live without fear, and to wait with hope and courage. He is certain that God will deliver him from his enemies.

WEEK 3, DAY 1

Absorb the passage in Psalm 27 by reading it aloud several times until you become familiar with its verses, words, and phrases.

WEEK 3, DAY 2

PSALM 27

The Setting

We cannot identify this psalm's original setting with any precision. While the temple in verse 4 may refer to the Jerusalem temple, the "sacred tent" seems to refer to the tabernacle—the place of worship before Solomon built the temple. The psalmist's reference to the "wicked," "enemies," "foes," and "false witnesses" may indicate a variety of situations. For example, if the psalmist were an ordinary Israelite, these references would refer to his personal enemies and those who tried to discredit him. Alternatively, because of the references to an "army" and "war," some commentators think the psalmist was an Israelite king. However, in verse 3, they seem to be introduced more as hypothetical situations than literal ones. Because worship in the temple usually included offering sacrifices, and some commentators think that in the original setting, the worshiper offered his sacrifice after declaring his confidence in God (verses 1–6; see "I will sacrifice" in verse 6). The reference to sacrifice is followed by a prayer for help (verses 7–14). "Wait for the Lord" (verse 14) may be the psalmist's own exhortation to himself or to others in similar crisis. Alternatively, a priest may have spoken this exhortation at the conclusion of the prayer for God's help.

The Organization

The psalm begins with the psalmist's confident statement and ends with an exhortation to wait for the Lord.

To discover the message of Psalm 27, let's divide the chapter into six sections. **Below, summarize or paraphrase the general message or theme of each grouping of verses (following the pattern provided for Psalm 27:1, 2–3, and 4–6).**

1. Psalm 27:1

The psalmist makes declarations about God and himself.

2. Psalm 27:2–3

The psalmist is confident amid serious threats to his life.

3. Psalm 27:4–6

The psalmist desires to experience God's presence and enjoy its benefits.

4. Psalm 27:7–10

5. Psalm 27:11–12

6. Psalm 27:13–14

WEEK 3, DAY 3

What's Happening in the Passage?

As we read through these passages, there are certain ideas and words that were familiar to the original readers, but are not as familiar to us. Two thousand years and a vastly different culture obscure some of these ideas from us today. You may encounter some of these words and ideas in your study today. Some of them have been explained in more detail in the **Word Study Notes**. If you want even more detail, you can supplement this study with a Bible dictionary or commentary.

1. Psalm 27:1

The psalmist acknowledges that God is his light, his salvation[1], and his stronghold;[2] he asserts that he does not live in fear of anything or anyone.[3]

2. Psalm 27:2-3

The psalmist expresses his trust[1] in God to keep him safe from all enemy attacks. He compares the threats of wicked people to a wild animal's attempt to devour its prey; an army's siege against a powerless city; and a war waged against him. He is confident that his enemies will suffer the same destruction they have plotted for him.

3. Psalm 27:4-6

Though troubles surround him, the psalmist does not complain or cry out for help, but earnestly seeks an ongoing experience of God's intimate presence.[1] As he comes to worship God in the temple, he is intentional about experiencing this presence and reflecting on God's graciousness, and hopes that this experience will continue through all of his life. The psalmist knows that God's presence, the temple, is his safe place in times of trouble. He does not claim to be self-sufficient, but seeks refuge in God's protective presence.[2] This safety gives him the courage to face his enemies because he is certain of his victory over them.[3] Anticipating God's help and deliverance, the psalmist pledges to offer a sacrifice of thanksgiving accompanied by joyful songs of praise.

45

WORD STUDY NOTES #1

[1] "My light and my salvation" are parallel expressions. In the Bible, light is often a metaphor for salvation and blessing. These expressions convey the psalmist's faith that God rescues those who trust in him from the power of darkness.

[2] "Stronghold" has military connotations; this is a place of safety, security, and protection from enemy attacks.

[3] "Whom shall I fear," and "of whom shall I be afraid" are rhetorical questions; they express the psalmist's decision to live fearlessly because of his trust in God.

WORD STUDY NOTES #2

[1] "I will be confident" conveys the psalmist's certainty that his enemies will fail in their attempts to destroy him because he trusts in God—the source of his life and salvation.

WORD STUDY NOTES #3

[1] Here, to "gaze on the beauty of the LORD" means to reflect on God's favor and graciousness.

[2] God is often portrayed in the psalms as the "rock"—the firm and reliable source of strength and protection for his people.

[3] "My head will be exalted" conveys the idea of the psalmist's victory over his enemies.

WORD STUDY NOTES #4

[1] In Israelite tradition, it is impossible to see God's face (see Exodus 33:20). Therefore, the three instances of "face" in these verses are figurative—seeking God's face means seeking God's intimate presence.

[2] In the psalms, appeals like the one in verse 9 are usually the psalmist's acknowledgement that his troubles are a sign of God's judgment. The psalmist does not mention a specific sin here; however, he seems to be burdened with guilt.

WORD STUDY NOTES #5

[1] The "straight path" is the path of righteousness—the opposite of the evil path that the psalmist's oppressors take.

[2] Ancient Israel's justice system depended on the integrity of witnesses. "False witnesses" pervert justice; in these cases, innocent people have no recourse but to appeal to God.

WORD STUDY NOTES #6

[1] "The goodness of the Lord" is the essence of God, or his fundamental nature (see Exodus 33:19-20).

[2] "The land of the living" is where one can enjoy the fullness of God's blessings.

[3] In the Old Testament, "to wait for the LORD" is not to remain passive but to hopefully anticipate and, thus, actively trust in God.

Create your own brief summary or description of the realities portrayed in verses 7–10, 11–12, and 13–14.

4. Psalm 27:7–10[1, 2]

_____

_____

_____

_____

_____

_____

_____

5. Psalm 27:11–12[1, 2]

_____

_____

_____

_____

_____

_____

_____

6. Psalm 27:13–14[1, 2, 3]

_____

_____

_____

_____

_____

_____

_____

Discoveries

Let's summarize our discoveries from Psalm 27.

1. The psalmist fearlessly trusts God to save him from his enemies.

2. The psalmist earnestly seeks to abide in God's presence forever.

3. The psalmist promises to offer a thanksgiving sacrifice and joyful songs to God for answering his prayer.

4. As he declares his commitment to serve God and walk in God's ways, the psalmist is confident that he will experience God's goodness.

5. The psalmist exhorts the worshiping community to wait with courage and anticipate God's goodness in their own lives.

Psalms of Trust and the Story of God

Whenever we read a biblical text, it is important to ask how it relates to the rest of the Bible. The themes of God as the savior and protector of his people; seeking God's presence; God's faithfulness; living with courage and hope; victory over enemies; and waiting for the Lord are themes found in many biblical texts. We also see the psalmist's hope for God's salvation realized through the death and resurrection of Jesus the Messiah. **In the space provided, write a short summary of how the themes of salvation and trust in God are reflected in each passage.**

1. Joshua 1:6

_____

_____

_____

_____

2. Psalm 24:5–6

_____

_____

_____

_____

3. Psalm 91:1–8

_____

_____

_____

_____

_____

If you have a study Bible, it may have references in a margin, a middle column, or footnotes that point to other biblical texts. You may find it helpful in understanding how the whole story of God ties together to look up some of those other scriptures from time to time.

4. Isaiah 60:1–2

_____

_____

_____

_____

_____

_____

_____

5. Matthew 26:59–60

_____

_____

_____

_____

_____

_____

_____

_____

6. John 1:4–5

_____

_____

_____

_____

_____

_____

_____

_____

_____

7. Acts 23:11

_____
_____
_____
_____
_____
_____
_____
_____
_____
_____
_____
_____
_____

8. 1 Corinthians 16:13

_____
_____
_____
_____
_____
_____
_____
_____
_____
_____
_____
_____
_____
_____
_____
_____

Psalms and Our World Today

When we look at the theme of trust in God in Psalm 27, it can become the lens through which we see ourselves, our world, and God's action in our world today.

1. What does this psalm tell us about dealing with fear?

It reminds us that trust in God is essential to dispelling our fears: fear of enemies, opposition, and threatening situations.

Following the above example, answer these questions about how we can understand our world, God's action, and ourselves.

2. In times of trouble (hostility, false accusations, illness, etc.), what do you normally do?

3. What do you seek to accomplish through the act of corporate worship?

4. How confident are you in God's faithfulness to you and his presence in your life?

_____

_____

_____

_____

_____

_____

_____

_____

_____

_____

_____

_____

5. How do you see yourself in light of the psalmist's admonition, "Wait for the Lord; be strong and take heart"?

_____

_____

_____

_____

_____

_____

_____

_____

_____

_____

_____

_____

_____

Invitation and Response

God's Word always invites a response. Think about the way the theme of trust in God speaks to us today. How does Psalm 27 invite us to respond?

_____

_____

_____

_____

_____

_____

_____

_____

_____

_____

_____

Praying the psalms is an important and meaningful spiritual discipline. Write your own prayer of trust using ideas and words found in Psalm 27.

_____

_____

_____

_____

_____

_____

_____

_____

_____

_____

_____

Trust in God is essential to
dispelling our fears.

PSALM 2

Scholars classify Psalm 2 as a royal psalm that was used during the coronation of kings from David's line. Royal psalms are characterized by references to God's "anointed" (*mashiach* or messiah). Psalm 2 focuses on God exercising his sovereign rule and authority over the nations through his anointed one.

Though this psalm has no introductory statement, it is a part of the Davidic psalms series (Psalms 1–41). Scholars often pair it with Psalm 1 and view them together as the introduction to the book. They find the first link between the two psalms in the pronouncement of blessing ("Blessed") found at the beginning of Psalm 1 and at the conclusion of Psalm 2. Psalm 1 instructs Israelite believers to live by meditating on God's instructions (*torah*); in Psalm 2, God's anointed instructs the rulers of the earth to live in submission to God's sovereign rule through him. Psalm 1 declares that the wicked are destined for destruction; Psalm 2 declares that rebellious rulers will face the same fate. Both psalms promise blessings to those who live in obedience to God. Together, these two psalms capture the invitation of the entire book of Psalms: to live in obedience to God's instructions.

The New Testament appropriates two features of this psalm in describing Jesus as the Son of God (see Mark 1:11; 9:7), and in describing the world's opposition to God's reign through him (Acts 4:25–27). For this reason, Christians categorize this as a messianic psalm and relate the words of the psalmist to the life and ministry of Jesus.

55

WEEK 4, DAY 1

Absorb the words of Psalm 2 as you read it aloud several times until you become familiar with its verses, words, and phrases.

WEEK 4, DAY 2

PSALM 2

The Setting

Some commentators think that this psalm reflects the coronation of a Davidic king. In the ancient world, revolts against newly enthroned kings (whether by internal or external forces) were frequent, and the opening verses indicate such a situation. As he envisions the universal reign of God through the newly anointed Davidic king, the psalmist also sees the coronation of this new king as the reason for the nations' and their rulers' rebellion against God's rule. In response, God asserts his sovereign authority and his relationship with the Davidic king through whom he rules the world.

The Organization

The psalm has a fairly straightforward structure. It begins with a rhetorical question and ends with a beatitude, a statement of blessing.

To discover the message of Psalm 2, let's divide it into four sections. **Below, summarize or paraphrase the general message or theme of each grouping of verses (following the pattern provided for 2:1–3 and 4–6).**

1. Psalm 2:1–3

A rhetorical question implies that the nations' conspiracy to rebel against God and his

anointed is futile.

2. Psalm 2:4–6

God responds mockingly to the rebel kings and declares his authority.

3. Psalm 2:7–9

_____

_____

_____

_____

_____

_____

_____

_____

_____

_____

_____

_____

_____

4. Psalm 2:10–12

_____

_____

_____

_____

_____

_____

_____

_____

_____

_____

_____

_____

_____

_____

_____

What's Happening in the Passage?

As we read through these passages, there are certain ideas and words that were familiar to the original readers, but are not as familiar to us. Two thousand years and a vastly different culture obscure some of these ideas from us today. You may encounter some of these words and ideas in your study today. Some of them have been explained in more detail in the **Word Study Notes**. If you want even more detail, you can supplement this study with a Bible dictionary or commentary.

1. Psalm 2:1–3

The nations and their rulers[1] are united in their conspiracy and rebellion against God's sovereign rule through his messiah.[2] This rebellion against God's rule is worldwide in scope. The rebel kings seek to gain freedom from God's reign. The psalm asserts the futility of any attempt to seek freedom from God's sovereign rule over the world.

2. Psalm 2:4–6

As God the heavenly ruler laughs at the futility of the earthly rulers' schemes, he also rebukes the rebels and expresses his anger toward them.[1] His speech causes terror and fear in the rebels who are opposed to his rule. God remains firm and declares the installation of his king[2] on Zion, his holy mountain.[3]

WORD STUDY NOTES #1

[1] "Kings" and "rulers" indicate that opposition to God's rule comes from powerful people in the world. They claim sovereignty and subject themselves to neither human nor divine authority.

[2] "Anointed" is *mashiach* in Hebrew ("messiah" in English; *Christos* [Christ] in Greek).

WORD STUDY NOTES #2

[1] "Anger" and "wrath" are manifestations of God's displeasure; they indicate a controlled emotion, the goal of which is not punishment, but to warn the rulers of the consequence of their rebellion.

[2] God's declaration of installing his king on Zion implies a coronation ritual in the temple. This statement may be understood as God's approval of the Davidic king's coronation.

[3] Jerusalem, the location of the temple, is often called Zion in poetic passages of the Bible.

Create your own brief summary or description of the realities portrayed in verses 7–9 and 10–12.

3. Psalm 2:7–9[1, 2, 3, 4]

_____

_____

_____

_____

_____

_____

_____

_____

_____

_____

_____

_____

4. Psalm 2:10–12[1, 2, 3]

_____

_____

_____

_____

_____

_____

_____

_____

_____

_____

WORD STUDY NOTES #3

[1]"I" and "me" in verse 7 refer to God's anointed (the Davidic descendant whom God installed as king in verse 6).

[2]"You are my son" indicates God's adoption of the Davidic king as his son (though this adoption does not mean that the human king became divine). 2 Samuel 7:14 also refers to the father-son relationship between God and the Davidic kings.

[3]"I have become your father" is a legal statement of adoption.

[4]With the phrase "dash them to pieces like pottery," the psalmist seems to draw imagery from the ancient royal custom of a newly enthroned king displaying his power by using his iron scepter to smash clay figures representing neighboring kings.

WORD STUDY NOTES #4

[1] "Serve the LORD with fear" sums up the wisdom instruction in the Old Testament (see Proverbs 1:7). "Serve the Lord" is a call to submission and service through worship.

[2]"With trembling" indicates that God's worshipers should have an attitude of humility.

[3]Commentators are uncertain about the meaning of the admonition, "Kiss his son." Some translations instead say, "Kiss his feet" because this image reflects the ancient custom of vassals prostrating themselves before a sovereign king. In the ancient world, kissing was a gesture of peacemaking and reconciliation. Both of these ideas (submission and reconciliation) fit well in this context.

Discoveries

Let's summarize our discoveries from Psalm 2.

1. Nations and kings oppose God's sovereign rule over the world through his anointed ruler.

2. God laughs at, chastises, and terrifies those who oppose to his sovereign rule.

3. God adopts his chosen king as his son and places him on the throne.

4. The world's rulers must live in submission to God and his anointed or else be destroyed.

5. Those who take refuge under God's sovereign rule will be blessed.

Royal Psalms and the Story of God

Whenever we read a biblical text, it is important to ask how it relates to the rest of the Bible. God's sovereign rule over the world is an emphasis found throughout Scripture. In the Old Testament, God chooses King David and his descendants to be the earthly agents of his sovereign rule. In the New Testament, the focus shifts to God's kingdom through Jesus Christ, the Son of God, and a descendant of David. The New Testament also anticipates Christ's eschatological reign over the world. **In the space provided, write a short summary of how the themes of God's sovereignty and God's anointed one are reflected in each passage.**

1. Psalm 22:27–28

_____

_____

_____

_____

_____

_____

_____

_____

2. Psalm 89:19–23

_____

_____

_____

_____

_____

_____

_____

If you have a study Bible, it may have references in a margin, a middle column, or footnotes that point to other biblical texts. You may find it helpful in understanding how the whole story of God ties together to look up some of those other scriptures from time to time.

61

3. Proverbs 1:24–26

_____
_____
_____
_____
_____
_____
_____
_____
_____

4. Matthew 28:18–20

_____
_____
_____
_____
_____
_____
_____
_____

5. John 5:22–23

_____
_____
_____
_____
_____
_____
_____
_____
_____
_____

6. Acts 13:32–33

7. Philippians 2:6–11

8. Hebrews 12:28–29

Psalms and Our World Today

When we look at the theme of God's sovereign rule in Psalm 2, it can become the lens through which we see ourselves, our world, and God's action in our world today.

1. According to Psalm 2, in what way does God give rebellious world rulers an opportunity to repent?

God warns the nations of the consequence of their continued rebellion against his sovereign rule.

Following the above example, answer these questions about how we can understand our world, God's action, and ourselves.

2. What do you see as evidence of rebellion against God's rule in our world?

3. What sort of life and conditions do you expect to see in a nation that is totally yielded to God's sovereign rule?

4. What sort of life and conditions do you expect to see in a community of faith that is totally yielded to God's sovereign rule?

_____

_____

_____

_____

_____

_____

_____

_____

_____

_____

_____

_____

5. What sort of life and characteristics do you expect to see in a person who is totally yielded to God's sovereign rule?

_____

_____

_____

_____

_____

_____

_____

_____

_____

_____

_____

_____

_____

Invitation and Response

God's Word always invites a response. Think about the way the themes of God's rule and God's chosen Messiah speak to us today. How does Psalm 2 invite us to respond?

_____

_____

_____

_____

_____

_____

_____

_____

_____

_____

_____

Praying the psalms is an important and meaningful spiritual discipline. Write your own prayer about God's rule using ideas and words found in Psalm 2.

_____

_____

_____

_____

_____

_____

_____

_____

_____

_____

_____

_____

Those who take refuge under God's sovereign rule will be blessed.

PSALM 49

Psalm 49 is a wisdom psalm that aims to provide instruction about what really matters in life. Old Testament wisdom instructions compare two ways of life: the righteous life, which is lived in the "fear of the Lord;" and the wicked life, which is lived on one's own terms. In this psalm, the psalmist contrasts wealth with poverty to show that wealth cannot save anyone from death; only God can do that.

This psalm is among those attributed to the Korahites (see the headings of Psalms 42, 44-49), who performed various services in the temple, including singing during public worship services (see 1 Chronicles 9:19; 2 Chronicles 20:19). The Korahite collection of psalms contains corporate prayers, songs, hymns, and wisdom instructions. "For the director of music" is probably an instruction for leading the singing of this psalm.

WEEK 5, DAY 1

Absorb the passage in Psalm 49 by reading it aloud several times until you become familiar with its verses, words, and phrases.

PSALM 49

The Setting

Though wisdom psalms do not often indicate how they were used in temple worship, verse 4 suggests that this psalm was probably sung in the temple accompanied by the harp. Verses 1–3 invite all peoples in the world, regardless of their socioeconomic status, to hear this song's words of wisdom. Thus, though this song was sung at the temple, it was meant for a worldwide audience.

The Organization

The overall message of this psalm is that riches have no power over death. The psalmist emphasizes that neither wealth nor those who trust in their wealth will endure; God alone has power over life and death.

To discover the message of Psalm 49, let's divide it into seven sections. **Below, summarize or paraphrase the general message or theme of each grouping of verses (following the pattern provided for 49:1–4, 5–6, and 7–9).**

1. Psalm 49:1–4

The psalmist invites everyone in the world to hear his words of wisdom.

2. Psalm 49:5–6

The psalmist does not fear evil days.

3. Psalm 49:7–9

The psalmist asserts that the rich cannot hope to live forever by the power of their wealth.

4. Psalm 49:10–12

5. Psalm 49:13–15

6. Psalm 49:16–17

7. Psalm 49:18–20

WORD STUDY NOTES #1

[1] "Low and high" is more literally translated "children of a human being and children of a man." In this context, "human being" means an ordinary individual, or a poor one; "man" means a person of influence and wealth.

[2] The "heart" is the seat of human emotions, thoughts, feelings, and perceptions. According to Psalm 37:30-31, "the law," or God's instruction (*torah*), is in the heart of the righteous who speak wisdom.

[3] Proverb (*mashal* in Hebrew) is a literary form found in the Old Testament. *Mashal* has many meanings; here, it seems to indicate instruction through comparison (see verses 12 and 20, in which the wealthy are likened to the beasts; the proverb shows that they are alike in that they both die).

WORD STUDY NOTES #2

[1] "Wicked deceivers" could also be translated "the iniquity of my deceivers."

[2] "Trust in their wealth" suggests self-sufficiency and self-reliance as opposed to dependence on God.

WORD STUDY NOTES #3

[1] The law stipulated that if a person was deemed responsible for his bull goring someone, he may escape the death penalty and redeem his own life with an appropriate ransom payment (see Exodus 21:28-30). However, this provision did not mean the person's claim upon his life was equal to God's— God still has the ultimate claim.

WEEK 5, DAY 3

What's Happening in the Passage?

As we read through these passages, there are certain ideas and words that were familiar to the original readers, but are not as familiar to us. Two thousand years and a vastly different culture obscure some of these ideas from us today. You may encounter some of these words and ideas in your study today. Some of them have been explained in more detail in the **Word Study Notes**. If you want even more detail, you can supplement this study with a Bible dictionary or commentary.

1. Psalm 49:1–4

The psalmist invites everyone in the world—people of low and high status,[1] the poor and the rich alike—to hear his words of wisdom. He means for his words to impart instruction and understanding to his audience. These words of wisdom come from the psalmist's heart.[2] The psalmist seeks to convey wisdom through a proverb,[3] which will take the form of a riddle. The proverb will be delivered by a song with the accompaniment of the harp.

2. Psalm 49:5–6

The psalmist is not afraid of evil days, though he has encountered them. He is surrounded by the wicked who deceive him.[1] His enemies do not trust God; they place their trust in their wealth.[2] They are proud and arrogant; they view themselves as the sole creators of their wealth. Though the psalmist views himself as a victim of their oppression, he knows there is no need to fear them.

3. Psalm 49:7–9

The psalmist understands that no one can redeem[1] another person's life or pay a ransom to God so that they can live forever. No amount of money is enough for God to give up his claim on human life. The psalmist describes death and decay as inescapable realities.

Create your own brief summary or description of the realities portrayed in verses 10–12, 13–15, 16–17, and 18–20.

4. Psalm 49:10–12[1, 2]

_____

_____

_____

_____

_____

_____

_____

_____

_____

_____

_____

_____

_____

WORD STUDY NOTES #4

[1] "Their tombs will remain their houses" is based on the Greek translation; in Hebrew, the line reads, "in their thoughts their houses will remain."

[2] "Though they had named lands after themselves" refers to people making legal transactions to claim ownership of property.

5. Psalm 49:13–15[1, 2]

_____

_____

_____

_____

_____

_____

_____

_____

_____

_____

_____

_____

WORD STUDY NOTES #5

[1] "The upright will prevail over them" implies the ultimate victory of those who trust in God over those who reject God. "In the morning" may refer to the time of awakening—the time appointed for the judgment of the wicked.

[2] "God will redeem me from the realm of the dead [sheol]" may refer to either deliverance from death or being raised from the grave. The latter (anticipation of resurrection or afterlife) seems more likely and is supported by the last line of verse 15 ("he will surely take me to himself").

6. Psalm 49:16–17[1]

_____

_____

_____

_____

_____

_____

_____

_____

_____

_____

_____

_____

_____

_____

7. Psalm 49:18–20[1]

_____

_____

_____

_____

_____

_____

_____

_____

_____

_____

_____

_____

_____

_____

_____

_____

Discoveries

Let's summarize our discoveries from Psalm 49.

1. God's wisdom teaches us how to live fearlessly in the midst of evil days brought on by those who trust in their wealth.

2. Death is the great equalizer; the wise and the unwise, the rich and the poor, will all die, and no one can escape death by paying a ransom.

3. God will redeem those who trust in him, and they will live in his presence.

4. Death will lead those who trust in themselves to their grave, where they will remain forever.

5. Those who trust in God have no need to live in fear of other people's wealth and splendor.

6. The wealthy who do not heed words of wisdom will die without hope of an afterlife.

Wisdom Psalms and the Story of God

Whenever we read a biblical text, it is important to ask how it relates to the rest of the Bible. Death as humanity's destiny is a theme we find in a number of biblical passages. In the New Testament, God demonstrates his desire to redeem us from death and decay by sending Jesus and raising him from the grave. **In the space provided, write a short summary of how the themes of human mortality, fear of God, and hope for life after death are reflected in each passage.**

1. Psalm 37:1–7

_____

_____

_____

_____

2. Psalm 52:1–7

_____

_____

_____

_____

3. Psalm 78:1–3

_____

_____

_____

_____

If you have a study Bible, it may have references in a margin, a middle column, or footnotes that point to other biblical texts. You may find it helpful in understanding how the whole story of God ties together to look up some of those other scriptures from time to time.

4. Ecclesiastes 2:16, 18

_____

_____

_____

_____

_____

_____

_____

_____

5. Matthew 6:19–21

_____

_____

_____

_____

_____

_____

_____

_____

6. Mark 10:17–22

_____

_____

_____

_____

_____

_____

_____

_____

7. Luke 12:16–21

_____

_____

_____

_____

_____

_____

_____

_____

_____

_____

_____

_____

_____

_____

8. 1 Timothy 2:5–6

_____

_____

_____

_____

_____

_____

_____

_____

_____

_____

_____

_____

_____

_____

_____

WEEK 5, DAY 5

Psalms and Our World Today

When we look at the theme of God's wisdom in Psalm 49, it can become the lens through which we see ourselves, our world, and God's action in our world today.

1. According to Psalm 49, why do so many people reject words of wisdom?

As the psalmist explains, our world is dominated by self-sufficiency, self-glorification, and pride; those who trust in themselves and their wealth are not interested in hearing godly wisdom.

Following the above example, answer these questions about how we can understand our world, God's action, and ourselves.

2. In what ways do people in our day attempt to "buy" and prolong life?

3. How does our world view the wealthy?

4. How do most people around you view death—with fear or hope? What is the basis of their fear or hope?

_____

_____

_____

_____

_____

_____

_____

_____

_____

_____

_____

_____

5. How do *you* view death? What is the basis for your own fear or hope?

_____

_____

_____

_____

_____

_____

_____

_____

_____

_____

_____

_____

_____

Invitation and Response

God's Word always invites a response. Think about the way the themes of wisdom, death, and hope speak to us today. How does Psalm 49 invite us to respond?

_____

_____

_____

_____

_____

_____

_____

_____

_____

_____

_____

Praying the psalms is an important and meaningful spiritual discipline. Write your own prayer of wisdom using ideas and words found in Psalm 49.

_____

_____

_____

_____

_____

_____

_____

_____

_____

_____

_____

_____

God's wisdom teaches
us how to live fearlessly
in the midst of evil days
brought on by those
who trust in their wealth.

PSALM 31

Psalm 31 is a personal lament punctuated by statements of confidence and trust. Personal laments usually begin with a prayer for help and a description of the crisis, followed by a concluding statement of trust. In this psalm, we find three appeals alternating with three statements of trust. The psalm then concludes with the psalmist's exhortation to the community of faith.

Psalm 31 occupies a special place in Christian tradition because of Jesus's use of verse 5 ("Into your hands I commit my spirit;" see Luke 23:46) during his final moments on the cross. This psalm is a regular part of scripture readings during Holy Week.

WEEK 6, DAY 1

Absorb the passage in Psalm 31 as you read it aloud several times until you become familiar with its verses, words, and phrases.

WEEK 6, DAY 2

PSALM 31

The Setting

This psalm contains numerous references to the dire conditions the psalmist faces and his desperate need for God's deliverance. He is afflicted with an illness which causes his body to weaken; his neighbors and even his closest friends treat him with contempt and horror. His life is endangered by a plot against him; he is the object of false accusations. In the midst of all these troubles, he trusts God to be his refuge and prays for God's deliverance. Ultimately, God answers his prayer.

The lament psalms (of which there are over fifty) indicate that worshipers in ancient Israel brought their petitions and pleas for God's help to the temple as part of their worship. As we see in verses 21–24, it was also customary for worshipers to return to the temple and publicly acknowledge God's answers to their prayers for deliverance. This psalm would have served as a model for other worshipers who faced similar crises. Jesus's use of a portion of verse 5 and the use of verse 13 in Jeremiah 20:10 demonstrate the psalm's influence upon God's people.

The Organization

The psalm is organized around the theme of trusting God and seeking his help in the midst of trials. The psalm develops this theme with prayers for help followed by statements of trust.

To discover the message of Psalm 31, let's divide it into seven sections. **Below, summarize or paraphrase the general message or theme of each grouping of verses (following the pattern provided for 31:1–5, 6–8, and 9–13).**

1. Psalm 31:1–5

The psalmist seeks refuge in God and pleads with God to deliver him from his enemies.

2. Psalm 31:6–8

The psalmist expresses his trust in the Lord, who has not abandoned him.

3. Psalm 31:9–13

The psalmist describes his physical and emotional crisis and his enemies' attempts to destroy

him as he prays for God's mercy.

4. Psalm 31:14

_____

_____

_____

_____

_____

_____

5. Psalm 31:15–18

_____

_____

_____

_____

_____

_____

6. Psalm 31:19–22

_____

_____

_____

_____

_____

_____

7. Psalm 31:23–24

_____

_____

_____

_____

_____

_____

WORD STUDY NOTES #1

[1] The psalmist did not wish to suffer shame as a person rejected by his own God, or a person who trusted in a God who could not save.

[2] The metaphors the psalmist uses to describe God (including "rock," "fortress," "refuge," etc.) convey the psalmist's trust in God for his defense and protection.

[3] God's name—known to Israel as Yahweh—conveys his character as a God of justice, righteousness, faithfulness, mercy, love, and compassion.

[4] "Spirit" (*ruach* in Hebrew) means wind, breath, or life. "Hands" symbolize strength and power. Thus, by committing his spirit into God's hands, the psalmist trusts in God's power to save him.

WORD STUDY NOTES #2

[1] The Hebrew term *hesed* (here translated "your love"; often translated "love," "mercy," "steadfast love," "unfailing love," etc.) denotes God's covenant loyalty and faithfulness.

[2] The psalmist uses the language of Exodus 3:7-8 to describe God's rescue.

WORD STUDY NOTES #3

[1] The psalmist may be using hyperbolic language in verses 9-10 to describe the intensity of his physical and emotional distress.

[2] "Broken pottery" describes something useless or worthless.

[3] "Terror on every side" (a phrase also found in Jeremiah 6:25; 20:3, 10; 46:5; 49:29) suggests being surrounded by danger.

What's Happening in the Passage?

As we read through these passages, there are certain ideas and words that were familiar to the original readers, but are not as familiar to us. Two thousand years and a vastly different culture obscure some of these ideas from us today. You may encounter some of these words and ideas in your study today. Some of them have been explained in more detail in the **Word Study Notes**. If you want even more detail, you can supplement this study with a Bible dictionary or commentary.

1. Psalm 31:1-5

The psalmist seeks refuge in God and makes it clear that his honor and integrity depend upon God's deliverance.[1] He begs God to attend to his prayers for rescue, protection, guidance, and safety.[2] The psalmist confesses that God is a righteous and faithful God whose name conveys his character.[3] He commits his life into God's hands[4] and pleads for deliverance from his enemies.

2. Psalm 31:6-8

The psalmist strongly denounces those who worship idols that cannot save. He expresses his trust in the LORD. The psalmist rejoices in God's covenant loyalty and faithfulness[1] as demonstrated through his saving actions. God sees the psalmist's struggles and rescues him from his enemies, providing him security.[2]

3. Psalm 31:9-13

The psalmist appeals for God's mercy as he suffers intense physical and emotional distress. His sickness affects his whole being; it weakens him and fills him with sorrow, grief, and anguish.[1] His physical and emotional crisis is compounded by enemy attacks upon his life. His enemies have turned his neighbors, closest friends, and even strangers against him. Now he is an outcast—a forgotten person the world deems worthless.[2] He is surrounded by dangerous adversaries[3] who plot to kill him.

Create your own brief summary or description of the realities portrayed in verses 14, 15–18, 19–22, and 23–24.

4. Psalm 31:14[1]

_____

_____

_____

_____

_____

_____

_____

_____

_____

_____

WORD STUDY NOTES #4

[1] With the phrase, "You are my God," the psalmist acknowledges that he is a member of God's covenant people (see Exodus 20:2).

5. Psalm 31:15–18[1, 2]

_____

_____

_____

_____

_____

_____

_____

_____

_____

_____

_____

WORD STUDY NOTES #5

[1] "My times are in your hands" expresses the psalmist's total reliance upon God for his future.

[2] God's face symbolizes his presence. "Let your face shine on your servant" is an appeal for God's favor and acceptance.

WORD STUDY NOTES #6

[1] Given the focus of verse 19 (and what the psalmist seeks throughout the psalm), "the good things" most likely refers to safety and protection in God's presence rather than material prosperity.

[2] In verse 21, "his love" refers again to God's covenant loyalty and faithfulness (*hesed*).

6. Psalm 31:19–22[1, 2]

WORD STUDY NOTES #7

[1] "Faithful people" is a translation of the Hebrew word *Hasidim*, which derives from *hesed* (see Word Study Note #1 on 31:6–8 and Note #2 on 31:19–22). The term indicates that this people responds to God's *hesed* with faithfulness and love for him.

[2] "Take heart" is an exhortation to be courageous.

7. Psalm 31:23–24[1, 2]

Discoveries

Let's summarize some of our discoveries from Psalm 31.

1. The psalmist seeks refuge in God, the source of his strength, protection, and salvation.

2. The psalmist renounces those who trust in idols.

3. In intense physical and emotional distress, abandoned by enemies and friends alike who plot to kill him, the psalmist pleads for God's deliverance.

4. God demonstrates his covenant loyalty and faithfulness through his favor and salvation.

5. The psalmist predicts that his arrogant, lying enemies will be silenced by death.

6. The psalmist declares that those who fear the LORD will remain safe in the shelter of his presence.

7. The psalmist challenges all who hope in God for their salvation to love the LORD and be courageous.

If you have a study Bible, it may have references in a margin, a middle column, or footnotes that point to other biblical texts. You may find it helpful in understanding how the whole story of God ties together to look up some of those other scriptures from time to time.

Psalms of Lament and the Story of God

Whenever we read a biblical text, it is important to ask how it relates to the rest of the Bible. Descriptions of God as a refuge, rock, fortress, or deliverer appear in a number of other psalms, as do testimonies to God's covenant loyalty and faithfulness. Additionally, references to God's mercy, trust in God, hope in God's deliverance, and praise to God for his salvation appear in other biblical books. **In the space provided, write a short summary of how the themes of lament, deliverance, and praise are reflected in each passage.**

1. Exodus 34:6

_____

_____

_____

_____

_____

2. Psalm 4:5

_____

_____

_____

_____

_____

3. Psalm 6:2, 7

_____

_____

_____

_____

_____

4. Psalm 18:19

_____

_____

_____

_____

_____

_____

5. Psalm 22:6

_____

_____

_____

_____

_____

_____

6. Psalm 23:3

_____

_____

_____

_____

_____

_____

7. Psalm 25:2–3

_____

_____

_____

_____

_____

_____

8. Jeremiah 20:10

_____
_____
_____
_____
_____
_____
_____
_____
_____

9. Luke 23:46

_____
_____
_____
_____
_____
_____
_____
_____
_____

10. Acts 7:59

_____
_____
_____
_____
_____
_____
_____
_____
_____

Psalms and Our World Today

When we look at the theme of lament in Psalm 31, it can become the lens through which we see ourselves, our world, and God's action in our world today.

1. How does the world around us conceive of the ideas of protection and deliverance?

We live in a world in which most people trust in the military strength of their nations and the

power of their governments to protect, defend, and deliver them from the internal or

external forces that threaten their lives.

Following the above example, answer these questions about how we can understand our world, God's action, and ourselves.

2. What are the "worthless idols" to which people in our world cling for protection?

3. The psalmist, like Jeremiah and Jesus, faced contempt, rejection, isolation, and threats to his life. How would our modern world view these examples of faithfulness and trust in God?

4. How does the psalmist's view of God's faithfulness and trustworthiness compare to our secular world's perception of God?

_____

_____

_____

_____

_____

_____

_____

_____

_____

_____

5. The psalmist encouraged the worshiping community to love the Lord and be strong and courageous. How do the people of God respond to God's deliverance from troubles and trials today?

_____

_____

_____

_____

_____

_____

_____

_____

_____

_____

_____

Invitation and Response

God's Word always invites a response. Think about the way the themes of lament and deliverance speak to us today. How does Psalm 31 invite us to respond?

_____

_____

_____

_____

_____

_____

_____

_____

_____

_____

_____

_____

Praying the psalms is an important and meaningful spiritual discipline. Write your own prayer of lament using ideas and words found in Psalm 31.

_____

_____

_____

_____

_____

_____

_____

_____

_____

_____

_____

God demonstrates his covenant loyalty and faithfulness through his favor and salvation.

PSALM 51

Psalm 51 is another example of an individual's lament. It is also the fourth of the seven penitential psalms in the Christian tradition (6, 32, 38, 51, 102, 130, and 143). The most common features of these psalms are an acknowledgement of sin; God's judgment of sin and its effects; and pleas for God's mercy.

This psalm is best known for its theology. Though human sin is a prominent theme, the psalm's primary focus is on God's nature as a gracious, merciful, forgiving God who cleanses, transforms, and restores penitent sinners into a right relationship with himself. Consequently, this psalm has been an important source for the church's understanding of sin, repentance, justification, and sanctification. For this reason, this penitential prayer is traditionally part of the liturgy on Ash Wednesday and during the season of Lent.

WEEK 7, DAY 1

Absorb the passage in Psalm 51 by reading it aloud several times until you become familiar with its verses, words, and phrases.

PSALM 51

The Setting

The heading attributes this psalm to David. It also places it in the context of Nathan's indictment of David after the king committed adultery with Bathsheba (see 2 Samuel 12:1–15). In the original Hebrew, "a psalm of David" is literally, "a psalm to/for David." This raises the possibility that the psalm was composed by a poet who either dedicated it to David or wrote it according to David's instructions. There is also a good chance that David composed this psalm himself; notice how verse 4 ("Against you, you only, have I sinned") echoes David's confession to Nathan in 2 Samuel 12:13 ("I have sinned against the LORD"). Additionally, various expressions in the psalm acknowledge the gravity of David's sin and his heartfelt penitence.

It is likely the present version of Psalm 51 includes later additions to the original text. Namely, scholars consider verses 16–19 to be an addition to the original prayer for God's mercy and forgiveness. The Babylonians' destruction of the temple in 586 BCE resulted in the suspension of Israel's sacrificial worship, which resumed only after the exiled people returned and rebuilt the temple (515 BCE). Consequently, the exilic and post-exilic period in Israel produced prayers for Zion's prosperity and the rebuilding of Jerusalem's walls. Prayers for a "new heart" and "a steadfast spirit" also echo the promises found in Jeremiah and Ezekiel (see Jeremiah 24:7; Ezekiel 36:26–27). Thus, it is possible that the original psalm was expanded during or after the Babylonian exile. It is also likely that when temple worship was restored in 515 BCE, the present version of this psalm became a model penitential prayer for both individual worshipers and the entire congregation.

The Organization

Some of the key themes of this psalm are deep awareness of the gravity of sin; appeals for God's mercy; pleas for the restoration of relationship with God; release from guilt; commitment to praise God; and proper sacrifice.

To discover the message of Psalm 51, let's divide it into seven sections. **Summarize or paraphrase the general message or theme of each grouping of verses (following the pattern provided for 51:1–2, 3–6, and 7–9).**

1. Psalm 51:1–2

The psalmist appeals for God's mercy and compassion and seeks God's cleansing of his iniquity and sin.

2. Psalm 51:3–6

The psalmist confesses that he sinned against God and that God was righteous in judging his sin.

3. Psalm 51:7–9

The psalmist prays for God's forgiveness and for restoration of his relationship with God.

4. Psalm 51:10–12

5. Psalm 51:13–15

6. Psalm 51:16–17

7. Psalm 51:18–19

WEEK 7, DAY 3

What's Happening in the Passage?

As we read through these passages, there are certain ideas and words that were familiar to the original readers, but are not as familiar to us. Two thousand years and a vastly different culture obscure some of these ideas from us today. You may encounter some of these words and ideas in your study today. Some of them have been explained in more detail in the **Word Study Notes**. If you want even more detail, you can supplement this study with a Bible dictionary or commentary.

1. Psalm 51:1–2

The psalmist appeals to God's unfailing love and great compassion[1] as he pleads for the Lord's mercy and cleansing.[2] He recognizes that his forgiveness rests solely on God's abundant love and compassion. The psalmist also accepts personal responsibility for his transgression, iniquity, and sin.[3] He pleads for mercy and cleansing from his sins, indicating his desire for transformation and a restored relationship with God.

2. Psalm 51:3–6

The psalmist admits that he is aware of the transgressions he committed; he is continually aware of his sin. He also confesses that his sin is first and foremost against God[1] and is evil in God's sight. By confessing his sinfulness, the psalmist admits that he is under God's judgment, and that this proves God's right to be the judge of sinners. The psalmist acknowledges that he was born a sinner and that his contact with the world of sin began at the moment of his conception.[2] He states that God desires faithfulness from humans even before they are born, and that God taught him wisdom to live a life of faithfulness while he was in the womb (which he then rejected after his birth).

101

WORD STUDY NOTES #1

[1] "Compassion" (*rahamim*) conveys the sense of God's "motherly compassion"; the Hebrew word is linguistically related to the word for womb (*raham*), the seat of a mother's comfort and compassion for her child.

[2] The terms "wash" and "cleanse" derive from the vocabulary of Levitical law, which required unclean persons to be made clean through ritual cleansing before they could be admitted into the temple for worship (see Exodus 19:10; Leviticus 14).

[3] Transgression (*pesha*) means willful defiance of and rebellion against God. Iniquity (*awon*) conveys the idea of turning away, going astray, twisting, bending, or distorting. Sin (*hattat*) indicates missing the mark or failure and can refer to intentional or unintentional violation of God's commands.

WORD STUDY NOTES #2

[1] The psalmist does not exempt himself from accountability to other people for his sins against them. Every sin, regardless of its nature, is a violation of God's law, and affects our relationships with both God and others.

[2] "Sinful from the time my mother conceived me" (literally, "in sin my mother conceived me") implies that the psalmist was conceived with a disposition to rebel against God.

WORD STUDY NOTES #3

[1] Once again, the psalmist uses the language of priestly rituals for the cleansing of unclean persons (see Leviticus 14: 4, 6, 49, 51, 52; Numbers 19:18-19). Hyssop is a small bush which some have identified as the Syrian marjoram.

[2] "The bones you have crushed" communicates the psalmist's mental and physical distress under the weight of his sin and guilt.

[3] The hiding of God's face usually conveys his displeasure and rejection of someone. Here, by asking God to turn his face away from his sins, the psalmist is asking the Lord to be gracious to him.

WORD STUDY NOTES #4

[1] The verb "create" (*bara'*) appears in the Old Testament only in the context of God's activity; it is prominent in Genesis 1. The verb conveys the idea of God doing something new or bringing into existence something that previously did not exist.

[2] The mention of God's "Holy Spirit" is rare in the Old Testament (it appears only here and in Isaiah 63:10-11).

[3] The withdrawal of God's Spirit from someone means that the person will receive no forgiveness from God and will live without hope.

3. Psalm 51:7–9

The psalmist pleads for God's forgiveness by asking him to purify[1] him from the uncleanness of sin and wash away the stains of his sin. This appeal implies his confidence that God's forgiveness is effective and complete. The psalmist also seeks to hear God's word of mercy so that joy and gladness might replace his distress and agony.[2] He once again asks God to forgive him by hiding his face from his sins[3] and wiping away his iniquity.

Create your own brief summary or description of the realities portrayed in verses 10–12, 13–15, 16–17, and 18–19.

4. Psalm 51:10–12[1, 2, 3]

_____

_____

_____

_____

_____

_____

_____

_____

_____

_____

_____

_____

_____

_____

_____

5. Psalm 51:13–15[1,2]

_____

_____

_____

_____

_____

_____

_____

6. Psalm 51:16–17[1]

_____

_____

_____

_____

_____

7. Psalm 51:18–19[1]

_____

_____

_____

_____

_____

_____

_____

_____

_____

WORD STUDY NOTES #5

[1] "Your ways" refers to divine requirements for human conduct and behavior as expressed in God's commandments. In this context, the phrase encompasses God's response to sin and sinners, as well as God's forgiveness and restoration of sinners who plead for his mercy.

[2] "Open my lips" implies that the psalmist's lips were sealed off by his guilt; only God's forgiveness can break the seal of guilt and empower him to praise God.

WORD STUDY NOTES #6

[1] "You do not delight in sacrifice . . . you do not take pleasure in burnt offerings" is not a dismissal of sacrifice; rather, it indicates that sacrifice alone is not sufficient to receive God's mercy.

WORD STUDY NOTES #7

[1] "Prosper Zion . . . build up the walls of Jerusalem" indicates the desolation of Zion and the ruin of Jerusalem due to the Babylonian invasion of Jerusalem in 586 BCE.

Discoveries

Let's summarize our discoveries from Psalm 51.

1. The psalmist appeals to God's love and compassion and pleads for God to cleanse him from his sins.

2. The psalmist is conscious of his sins, takes responsibility for them, and submits to God's righteous judgment.

3. The psalmist's contact with sin began before his birth, yet even then, God offered him wisdom for faithful living.

4. The psalmist asks God to cleanse him from the impurities of sin, transform him, and renew his inner being so that he might live in conformity to God's will.

5. The psalmist begs God not to banish him from his presence and asks for a joyful awareness of God's salvation.

6. The psalmist recognizes that God does not accept sacrifices offered without genuine contrition and brokenness of heart.

7. The psalmist prays for the restoration of Zion and anticipates that righteous people will offer pleasing sacrifices to God in the restored temple.

WEEK 7, DAY 4

Psalms of Lament and the Story of God

Whenever we read a biblical text, it is important to ask how it relates to the rest of the Bible. God's unfailing love; sin and its effects; God's righteous judgment of sin; and God's forgiveness and cleansing from sin are themes found throughout the psalms and elsewhere in the Bible. **In the space provided, write a short summary of how the themes of lament, repentance, and mercy are reflected in each passage.**

1. Psalm 15:1–2

_____

_____

_____

_____

_____

_____

_____

2. Psalm 25:6–7

_____

_____

_____

_____

_____

_____

_____

_____

If you have a study Bible, it may have references in a margin, a middle column, or footnotes that point to other biblical texts. You may find it helpful in understanding how the whole story of God ties together to look up some of those other scriptures from time to time.

3. Isaiah 59:12–13

_____

_____

_____

_____

_____

4. Ezekiel 36:26–27

_____

_____

_____

_____

_____

5. Luke 15:21

_____

_____

_____

_____

_____

6. Romans 3:4–6

_____

_____

_____

_____

_____

7. Ephesians 4:30

_____
_____
_____
_____
_____
_____
_____
_____

8. Hebrews 9:14

_____
_____
_____
_____
_____
_____
_____

9. 1 John 1:7

_____
_____
_____
_____
_____
_____
_____
_____

WEEK 7, DAY 5

Psalms and Our World Today

When we look at the theme of lament in Psalm 51, it can become the lens through which we see ourselves, our world, and God's action in our world today.

1. How does our culture's understanding of repentance compare to what we see in Psalm 51?

We live in a world in which most people refuse to seek forgiveness from those they have

offended; instead, they try to justify or cover up their offenses. The confessions we hear in

media, courts, and even the church usually lack genuine contrition and deep sorrow over sin.

Following the above example, answer these questions about how we can understand our world, God's action, and ourselves.

2. What do most people think about their sin's effect on God and others?

3. How would our world react to the idea that God is righteous in his judgment?

4. According to this psalm, how does God totally transform (sanctify) those whose sins are forgiven?

_____

_____

_____

_____

_____

_____

_____

5. According to this psalm, what is the proper posture of a sinner who comes before God to worship him?

_____

_____

_____

_____

_____

_____

_____

6. According to this psalm, what is the appropriate response of a sinner who has been forgiven, cleansed from sin, transformed, and renewed by God?

_____

_____

_____

_____

_____

_____

_____

Invitation and Response

God's Word always invites a response. Think about the way the themes of contrition and forgiveness speak to us today. How does Psalm 51 invite us to respond?

_____

_____

_____

_____

_____

_____

_____

_____

_____

_____

Praying the psalms is an important and meaningful spiritual discipline. Write your own prayer of lament using ideas and words found in Psalm 51.

_____

_____

_____

_____

_____

_____

_____

_____

_____

_____

_____

_____

The portrayal of God as merciful and forgiving is a source of hope for all sinners who seek freedom from the power of sin.

www.ingramcontent.com/pod-product-compliance
Lightning Source LLC
Chambersburg PA
CBHW081538040426

42447CB00014B/3416